Items should be returned on or before the last date shown below. Items not already requested by other borrowers may be renewed in person, in writing or by telephone. To renew, please quote the number on the barcode label. To renew on line a PIN is required. This can be requested at your local library.
Renew online @ **www.dublincitypubliclibraries.ie**
Fines charged for overdue items will include postage incurred in recovery. Damage to or loss of items will be charged to the borrower.

Leabharlanna Poiblí Chathair Bhaile Átha Cliath
Dublin City Public Libraries

Dublin City
Baile Átha Cliath

Date Due	Date Due	Date Due

D1357550

Gallery Books
Editor Peter Fallon
LINER NOTES

Ciaran Berry

LINER NOTES

Gallery Books

Liner Notes
is first published
simultaneously in paperback
and in a clothbound edition
on 17 October 2018.

The Gallery Press
Loughcrew
Oldcastle
County Meath
Ireland

www.gallerypress.com

ISBN 978 1 91133 747 8 *paperback*
     978 1 91133 748 5 *clothbound*

A CIP catalogue record for this book
is available from the British Library.

Liner Notes receives financial assistance
from the Arts Council.

Contents

Once more, the sprockets turn, engage the spools —
    I've pressed record so that you can press play.
On the first track, side one, or the last, side two,
    once more, the sprockets turn, engage the spools.
In this jewel case, on this inlay card, for you:
    the song sequence of what I've tried to say.
Once more, the sprockets turn, engage the spools.
    I've pressed record so that you can press play.

for Leo and Aengus

Liner Notes

Because this song's made of the airwaves
a time machine you start to play the air
guitar of memory, making a country
so you can walk back into it, like a man
on rewind in a silent film, his whiskey tumbler
filling up again as he rises from his stool
and steps backwards towards the avenue
where the cars, cabs, trucks reverse away from him,
and the lights, for once, turn amber to green;
where the two hands on his watch unravel time,
like a maiden aunt unpicking a whole evening's worth
of knitting over the dropped stitch that means
she must go back before she can go on.
You raise the record from its sleeve again,
hold it grail-like into the wayward light
to read the liner notes on a life you've lived
all wrong. Wind in the sycamores outside,
rain coming down in a town you left behind
and not this one, where the backward longing
can strike you anytime — breath on the nape
of your neck when you're the only one in line,
cat with a broken spine dragging itself off
into the undergrowth; where the silence
might give way to a high-hat or snare drum,
the lub-dub of the bass, a brass section.
After a long absence you take up the thread again,
take up the line, what you listen for,
try not to listen for, stirring the tiny hairs
within your inner ear, weighting the wet tip
of your tongue, like the scuff and fumble
of the blind needle finding its way from silence
to the beginning of side one. You nod
your head 'yes'. You sing along. You tap
the steering wheel of the car in which you pass
under the strobes of stars, a quarter moon,

until, despite yourself, you are sixteen
again and walking home in a downpour
with your Ken Dodd quiff, your flowers of sulphur,
towards the box of records from which you'll pick
a tune to name the afternoon — its scattered
showers with a chance of sunny spells later,
its gust and bluster from Rathlin to Cape Clear.
This one would sound good in a stadium.
It's all guitar shimmer, tremolo arm,
a chorus that staggers smitten towards
the open bar. This one's a plea, a paean
on just six strings until the horns cut in,
like the bully at a prom. It recalls
the taste of cigarettes and bubblegum
on the tongue of the first girl you ever kissed.
All broken glass and bruised finger, its swoon
circles forever the turntable in that blue room
where you fed and watered every slight and scar.
And so you'd like to thank the engineer,
his assistant who provides the harmonies
and made the tea; the trumpet player,
his spit still wet in the mouth of a solo
the vinyl keeps pristine, black box recorder
to your submerged plane; the singer
with a bone caught in her throat, which is
another way to say longing; the producer,
who fills in on Hammond organ. You could
go on like this, lost in the noise again,
in your baroque joy at what was and is,
and what the words become, talking
to yourself in the second person, as if
you're fooling anyone, reading the liner notes
on a life you measure song by song.

Top of the Pops

There was either a message in a bottle
or a brown girl in the ring
when I squeezed my way between
Sister Áine and Sister Catherine
in the convent TV room.

Video may well have killed the radio star
but love was still in the air,
for so sang John Paul Young.
We didn't know then what might
be read into our favourite

exponent of the wobble board
tying his kangaroo down,
or what the glitter man might really
have meant when he asked,
'D'you wanna be in my gang?'

As far as those Sisters of Mercy
were concerned I was one
of their own, even if my father's whereabouts
were unknown Sunday mornings,
even if I would pass up

the chance to carry in the myrrh
and frankincense. Taking
a few pointers from The Pointer Sisters
or a guy down the chip shop
we watched as the second

would-be Welsh Elvis went weak
at the knees. 'I'll Be Satisfied'
was up to number nineteen
the same week 'I Don't Wanna Dance'
leapt from thirty to eleven.

We were either sitting by the rivers
of Babylon or we were walking
on the moon when Sister Pius
adjusted the rabbit ears and the countdown
continued from ten to one.

Foley

A horse was two cups tapped
                against a tabletop. A closed fist
        hitting bone was a closed fist
hitting bone. Now the foley
                of the past's awake again and hard
        at his mimetic work.

Not water diviner so much
                as white-faced mime plunging
        a hand into the lucky bag
of time, he conjures, from a fistful
                of cellophane, a scrim of rain;
        insect wings from a scrap

of sticky tape, a pocket fan.
                Your doppelgänger on the sound stage,
        your better looking twin, he tracks
your silent steps across the screen,
                where you're Guido led back blind
        towards who he's been,

or Daffy Duck breaking down
                the fourth wall to complain. Out of
        the clutter of typewriters, rotary
phones, a snorkeler's mask, a pair
                of wellingtons, he stirs sense
        of your every twist

and turn, wearing your boots to tread
                the boards, rubbing your winter coat
        against a microphone. He sets
a red foil fish onto your palm
                to tell your future by the heat
        beneath your skin,

and offers you the hardboiled sweets
          of the bygone that melt to soap
     and sugar on the tongue. The past
is bric-à-brac and hand-me-down,
          a thrift-store suit, a vagrant troupe
     of clowns, one on the tuba,

one on the clarinet. The past
          is kitsch stand-up, an irate duck
     railing against the mute maker
who keeps setting him up. In one scene
          you're that fêted musketeer
     swinging a sword

at barns and grain silos. In another
          you schlep through snow in a straw hat,
     a pair of dungarees, a mattock
slung over your right shoulder.
          And it's never far enough away,
     is it, your erasure,

the pencil's pink rubber turned towards
          your feathered form? While the foley,
     all feet and hands amidst his props,
sets and resets the metronome to mimic
          your meander, drops wet paper
     to make a sound like sick.

Extra Terrestrial

The flowers die, the flowers come back to life.
Through the rainbow blinds I point towards my lost star.
It's as if I'm that sad usher waving her torch
along the rows of the Astor Cinema to make sure
the courting couples haven't gone too far.
Crushed Coca-Cola cans, Monster Munch,
Sam Spudz Thicker Crimped Cheese 'n' Onion. The smell
of popcorn and of piss from the men's room.

I throw a ball into the dark, the ball comes back.
I step once more into the backyard of the film, light washing
through the slats of the unkempt garden shed.
Its rakes and hoes. Its charcoal and lawn seed.
I sit out in a deckchair, wait for whatever it is
to take a form. I leave a trail of Skittles or M&M's
on the off chance it might follow me home —
this creature who is me and not me I'll conceal

behind the bedroom closet's louvered doors,
his head nothing anyone would ever look for
amidst the one-eyed teddy bears and GI Joes.
The way his skin is stretched across his bones
puts me in mind of some ageing relative
whose veins begin to show through the translucence
like the curves and discursions of a back road.
Whin bushes and fuchsia, oak and ash, potholes.

A strip of grass running down the middle
like a Mo-Hick haircut as my aunt was wont to say
of what must be Dolan's Lane or Dolan's Brae.
I take the long way round again so as not to be seen
in my Lord Anthony coat and bell-bottom jeans.
His sacred heart, his telescopic limbs
remind me I'm space cadet, I'm alien,
a blow-in on my way home with messages.

Soup meat wrapped in brown paper. In waxed paper,
a sliced pan. A plastic bag of bones the dog
will bury in the ground where later we'll bury him.
I carry it all in the basket of my mother's Raleigh Shopper
that I wish were a BMX or a Chopper,
a flame motif across the double crossbar
on which my cousin, acting the goat, will split
his scrotum right between the stones. To think of it

is to cross your legs like that girl in the back row
who fears things are about to go too far,
her souped-up lover staring at the screen,
where those two brothers sniff the warp and weft
of their absent father's shirt for the scent
of Sea Breeze (or, is it, Old Spice?) as his hand
ascends the incline of her thigh. I lie down
beside it again, go eye to eye with it. The spilled milk

on the kitchen floor. The cold sweat on a can
of Coors. I finger the dial of that transmitter and receiver
conjured from a circular-saw blade, a record player,
the keyboard from a Speak & Spell. I hold
my ear up to this unlabeled baked bean tin
and hope you'll pick up at the other end
and talk to me along this piece of string. It's been too long,
and what I want now more than anything

is that moment when the bikes shift skywards
in a sudden swell of strings above the hillside
of the half-built suburban dream. Redwoods and cornfields.
The tinkle of a nearby stream. Everything
balanced on the handlebars and freewheeling,
like a boy kicking his Nikes or Adidas through midair.
The steady skitter of the reel. The tractor beam
of the projector. Before all of this puncture and repair.

How to Make a Snooker Table Laugh

I drop my fifty pence into the slot,
woodcock side up. The lights erupt
above the brushed rectangle of green baize.
My father racks the balls. I'm first to break.

The reds scatter like unpaired electrons,
or ping-pong balls discharged from a pop gun.
My father's trying to find a way around
the silence he never meant to pass down

to me. I sink the pink off the cushion
where, later, I'll try to split the atom
with a girl from the next town. The door kicked in.
The snooker hall gone to the wall by then.

I rub blue chalk over my cue's leather tip.
I make a bridge out of my thumb and fingertips.

Your Next One for Dancing

1

It was the year of the line dance and the Lada,
of slappin' leather and cheap Eastern Bloc cars,
the year the Marathon became the Snickers bar
and the Sinclair Spectrum the Commodore 64,
everything turning from black and white to colour,
from the petrol shortage and the Stardust fire
to the dirty protest of the last hunger striker —
ballot box in one hand, armalite in the other,
as it was in that and every other year
in which plain-clothes *gardaí* went door to door
looking first for Ben Dunne, then for Shergar,
and a checkpoint soldier, as we crossed the border,
asked my father first for his driver's licence,
then, if you wouldn't mind, sir, who shot JR?

2

And if you wouldn't mind, sir, who shot JR?
was the question in the bookmakers and bars.
Our neighbour gave birth to twins, a son and daughter
she named for that Cain figure and his trophy wife
the day Bobby came back to life in the shower.
I watched through the keyhole, or from behind a chair,
my mother having by then closed the door
since her favourite soap had barely passed the censor,
who'd shook his head 'no' to *Esprit* and *Hustler*
in the year of the Soda Stream and the karaoke singer
singing 'I Will Always Love You' and 'Jolene'
back-to-back in The Shamrock or The Anchor,
where it was country night, and your next one for dancing
was 'Drop Kick Me, Jesus (Through the Goalposts of Life)'.

3

Drop kick me, Jesus, through the goalposts of a life
in which I must go back in order to go on,
though I can't see if it's The Whirlwind or The Hurricane
who's about to make a break of one, four, seven
on the TV that hangs high above the lounge
in what must be the year of the Escort Mark III,
of the white stiletto and the Doc Marten,
a pocket-bound green kissing against the brown
as the Sunday afternoon crowd chase pints down
with a shot of John Power or a shot of John Jameson,
a Sweet Afton or a Carroll's Number One
while, in the arcade next door, a starved Pacman
eats the galaxy out of house and home,
and the jukebox lights up and splutters into song.

4

The jukebox lights up and splutters into song.
It must be something else love-stricken and love-torn.
A pedal steel solo. A brush of strings,
silver or phosphor bronze. Or something flush with keyboard
and drum machine, camp and new romantic,
bound up in its highlights, its dance routine —
an ode to the cocktail waitress or the funky town
like this one in the year of *Now 6* or *Now 7*,
of the six counties as British as Finchley
and the Reagans dropping in for tea at Ballyporeen,
of trickle-down economics that would trickle down
only as the acid rain augured from Cape Clear
to Valentia Island, Malin Head to Mizen,
and the snow, like a cataract, closing Ireland's Eye.

5

The snow like a cataract closing Ireland's Eye
which was forever looking the other way
through the dry ice, or the smoke of a Major
that would jaundice a little more the Barnesmore Gap
between its index and its middle finger
in the year of the bog butter and the butter voucher,
the slow cooker and the toasted sandwich maker,
the carriage clock, the wok, the egg timer,
the fondue set and, yes, of course, the cuddly toy
passing us once more on the conveyor
of a game show come to lighten the dark hours
between *The Angelus* and *The Six Million Dollar Man.*
What was Bully's special prize? Who was the mystery guest?
Whatever you remember you get to take home.

6

Whatever you remember you get to take home,
whether it's word of the weather or a dirty joke,
the day's score draws or its runners and riders
in the Chinese year of the rat or of the snake,
where every telephone pole from Ballybrit
to the Curragh wore an election poster for
the alleged sheep rustler or the alleged gun runner
of one Fianna or the other, like the penguin suit
and slip-on shoes my brother would wear,
bound for his prom, where the choice was roast beef
or turkey and ham before the band set off
on 'Highway to Hell' or 'Stairway to Heaven',
a slow set, then the lights turned back on:
'Would you all please stand for the national anthem?'

7

Would you all please stand for the national anthem,
then your zigzag stagger to the chip shop or the bus,
where you'll drop a hint and try to drop the hand
on your longhaired friend, who loves a Babycham,
who, on your dandruffed shoulder, will rest her perm
as you go first cheek to cheek, then chin to chin,
to the meek strains of 'Love is a Battlefield'
or 'Time After Time', before you lie down
together in a byre or barn? Blush once more
over your chat-up lines, all that ersatz banter,
as the mirror ball and dry ice give over
to the spilled lager light of dawn, Mizen Head
to Malin, Cape Clear to Bloody Foreland,
in the year of the Lada and the line dance.

For Shergar

Here's whip and stirrup, terret and blinker.
            Here's something stolen that I can't return.
        It's Epsom Downs or it's the Curragh of Kildare
where, with a sudden shift of gears, that makes
            him lift almost skyward, the odds-on favourite
        leaves behind a sluggish field.

Of course he brings the punters to their feet.
            Of course the commentator's short of words,
        his voice rising through the registers
as the jockey, in the green of the Aga Khan,
            rises almost to standing, and his mount breaks
        and enters the home straight.

Even to say his name those days was to invoke
            a myth with a white blaze on its forehead
        and one wobbly eye. And any old nag
anyway is so much rich vocabulary,
            just one hind leg made up of hock, fetlock,
        pastern and coronet.

If I watch this happen then it must be
            on a neighbour's colour set. An early
        Wednesday in June. A sitting room where the man
of the house rises from his chair to slap his thigh
            with an imaginary crop and call the horse
        in motion 'poetry'.

If I watch it again it must be because
            I measure out my life in hands, open its mouth
        to count its rotting teeth, knowing
everything we touch must turn to air.
            I'm ten. The horse stands in the winners'
        enclosure. The kettle boils.

Someone brings out the tea and custard creams,
            and I'm not sure if this is ode or elegy,
      or if the difference matters. Here's cannon
and coffin joint. Here's prophet's mark. The heart
            of a horse which weighs about the same
      as a newborn babe. Here are

the masked men who barge through the groom's door
            and steal the bay colt out under the winter stars.
      It's two years later. The wipers on my father's car
(A Simca? A Chrysler?) wave goodbye
            as we slosh through the rain behind the mover's van
      the same day my grandfather

leaves behind the broken stall of his body,
            his cancer too a sort of kidnapper. Days
      like that you learn to live a little more
in the language. Days like that you learn to love
            the names of things. Throatlatch and muzzle,
      poll and martingale,

how to say Shergar is to conjure stealth
            and speed, even if he becomes less and less
      himself and more the hieroglyph
for horse, horse simile. How to say the name,
            or how to hold it back, is to consider
      all that might disappear,

loaded into a livestock box and later shot
            and buried in the bog with oak roots, arrowheads,
      a broken spear. So much of it is objects
in the rearview mirror. So much of it is
            loss, its svelte dictions, the past tense
      entering its perfect form.

Here is my father's Chrysler inching north
            with a slow puncture. Here's the fistful of dirt
        I'll never scatter over that lowered box. Here's
the future, with a smoker's cough, calling
            to say we've got your horse. If you want proof
        we can send you an ear.

Heavy Metal

Lead, for instance, that rolled up lump of it I'd heft about
    the shed
hoping for biceps that might impress some Deirdre or Diane.

Later I tried a breezeblock, then a sledge. I stare up at the
    table
of elements again. Cobalt next to nickel. Zinc above cadmium.

Double Science before lunch. The bell rings or the voice
of the vice-principal comes across the intercom, its atomic
    weight,

its specific gravity kin to the tone my father's fourth or fifth
favourite TV detective was prone to assume when what had
    been

a mystery became clear to him — arsenic in the gruel
the plot device that had put paid to the country dentist's wife.

He'd have someone in the vice before too long, as I'd be held
    firm
in the grip of another detention where the chaplain would ask

the name of each internee's favourite band. Six AC/DCs. Five
Iron Maidens. A closed fist to your upper arm if you said
    Wham!

My Mother Meets The Rolling Stones

A clip from the archives will show their plane
landing at Aldergrove, the skittish screams of fans,
Keith's scissor wit on questions of the bowl cut,
Mick so articulate about the art of mime.
'What sort of image does your group present
to average dads and mums?' the interviewer asks,
prompting a smile, a shrug buttermilk sour.
Belfast's still black-and-white and thran and dour
as my mother puts aside her mascara
and leaves for a dance at their hotel where the air's rent
with reefer and spilled beer, and doing a line
will come to mean not romance but a white snuff
imbibed by a flapper from Amsterdam,
her breast exposed where Brian's signed his name.

Elvis Impersonator

In Phoenix, Amarillo, and Abilene,
              everyone waits downstairs for me to sing.
       I will go on after the last comedian,
swapping my hair shirt for this jumpsuit
           with rhinestones. I wait for the last gag
    to end, the one about ex-wives.

I wait for canned laughter, the rainfall
           of applause, that brief flutter I live for.
     As if each newborn came shadowed
by a stilled twin who must exist again
          in the shadow of his sibling, lost to
    Placidyl and Dexedrine,

I am the stand-in who stands clad in
           these storied hand-me-downs beneath
    the mirror ball's slow dance and spin. I am
the hind legs and spine of the pantomime
         horse, the rodeo clown squeezing into
    a pair of blue suede shoes

as the butter melts in your popcorn
           and you dream again of the drive-in,
    the beehive haircut and the Dairy Queen
in Wichita, South Bend, or Birmingham.
          In Tulsa, Tuscaloosa, or Des Moines,
    this is my foil, my put-on face.

And the truth? God's honest? I was so bored
          with being only myself, as we all are
    beneath the sunglasses, the spray-on tan,
behind the windows we cover with aluminum
         to block out the sun. Aloha from Hawaii,
    for the next while I'll be

your magpie thieving bright things from a nest
        not his own, your mockingbird wrapping his tongue
    around another's songs. So let's not forget
that Elvis Aaron barely wrote a thing,
        that I too could go gospel or country
    on a whim. Meanwhile,

I give you, one last time, my turned-up collar.
        I give you the doughnuts and the cheeseburgers
    and, in a Memphis theme park, the roller-
coaster I ride after hours alone. As my guitar
        player says, I'm all gut and fucked-up and I never
    leave the house without a gun.

The Death of Elvis

This lip, too, used to curl a little easier
and we, all of us, must enter our Vegas years.

Blessèd the pacemakers, blessèd the painkillers,
blessèd our famed quiffs grown flyaway, grown thin,

the grey starting to sprout under the dye.
So much to hide beneath the spit and mascara.

So much to powder puff and trim. Nose hairs,
for instance, and sideburns, the skin seasick

as we're made to play dress-up one final time.
A daughter's bracelet slipped over a wrist

and, for the ring finger, a lightning bolt ring.
How far we venture from a love of peanut butter

and Wonder Bread, how far from a Stutz Blackhawk
and Kahlil Gibran. From codeine, meperidine,

diazepam, the room with the teddy bears
and the empty syringe. How far

from the last book we dived into to learn
about sexual positions and astrological signs.

And far, too, from the myth of our baritones
coming alive in Tupelo, of how we could turn on

and off the rain. 'That's the way the mop flops,'
I think he'd say, as they lay him out flat

under the chandelier, then in the limousine.
'That's the way the mop flops,' as five men

enter his mausoleum with water, cement,
and a wheelbarrow full of sand,

the instruments set down, the stage lights dimmed,
'Thank you very much! Goodnight, Graceland.'

Shopping in Whole Foods on a Snowy Evening

If commerce, too, has its music, then it's in kumquat, pine
        nut, Arctic char,
    it's the squeaky front wheel of my little cart which
            seems to know the way
between the dry goods and the winter greens, and how my
        son says 'cookie'

    as he kicks me through his barred-in seat. All he craves
            these early days
is sugar, fat, the dark sweet mysteries of a chocolate chip.
        Outside, the snow
    does whatever it is snow does. Banks, I suppose, drifts,
        and perhaps swirls.

Throws a fresh sheet over the asphalt and the cars. Stretch
        out here, it seems
    to say. Lay down and make a pillow with your hands.
            And stopped forever
in those four quatrains, Frost's horse, his man, stand still and
        watch it fall

    between the pines, one seeing perhaps the rag tooth of
            his own gravestone,
the other winter with a bridle in its hand. The bell a Salvation
        Army worker
    rings has me thinking of them, the horse's nostrils
            steaming like a wet engine,

his master lost in his reverie, his swoon, and nothing to be
        done. His eyes
    on the snow, my eyes on him, like the eyes of the
            cameraman who can't seem
to drag his gaze away from those souls who, forsaken, climb
        the rails.

We're in San Francisco now and not this New England.
         Frost's hometown
until his father, a newspaperman, succumbs to the black
         lung. The bridge
      between the city and the bends of Highway 1, pressing
         north towards

Stinson Beach and Oregon. And it's here they come to jump
         — one buck-
      toothed in an early photograph who, a friend explains,
         was born an old man.
Black his clothes. Black his hair. Black his curtains. Black his
         plunge

      into the black of the ocean. One who, mid-fall, changes
         his mind and survives
black-boned, kept alive, he says, by a seal until the Coast
         Guard comes, a deed
      he claims as proof of his god's omnipotence. Sometimes
         I think the snow

is its own snuff movie, white of the mind after the world
         caves in. Lear
      on his heath charging not 'you elements'. Our traveller
         weary and wanting
to lie down. Sometimes I think it's a wedding dress, taken
         off, put on,

      raised from its sailor trunk in the attic where the moths
         have gotten in,
and where it sallows like old paper or old skin. The skin, let's
         imagine,
      about the bones of Frost's father as he swims towards a
         bell buoy at Pier 24,

leaving his son behind to mind his clothes. Now he turns to
    wave, and now
      he changes stroke. Later, at *The Evening Post*, the boy
        will find,
in his old man's desk drawer, bullets and a bottle of bourbon
    two thirds consumed.

      'I know San Francisco like my own face,' he'll tell an
        audience.
And of his father? 'I trailed him everywhere, in the way a
    boy does.'
      Who's to say, out of such loss, you might not conjure a
        horse, a man gazing

into the snow, as though it were nakedness, or the broken line
    down the middle
      of a midnight road? Who's to say you might not conjure
        a man seeking cake flour
and marshmallows before the first plough lowers the rupture
    of its blade?

      Have you ever felt your life become a film you are
        making, and you unable
to step out from behind the lens? Have you ever felt the cold
    gnaw at your bones
      knowing where your mind goes and what your hand has
        done? Before launching

his body water-ward, our saved boy downs a final meal of
    Starburst and Skittles,
      the colours making a sticky rainbow in his palm. A
        suspension bridge needs gravity
to stand, I've read somewhere. We hover between anchorage
    and mid-span.

Dolly

Maybe it's the telemetry of our telomeres
that for the tropes of country music makes us pine,

how we begin and end between the theme park and the pen,
in a one-bedroom next to The Wishy Washy

or a glass case in an Edinburgh museum,
our ideas of beauty patterned on the town tramp

or the Finn Dorset in its platonic form.
Always the lamb for which we'll lie down with the lion,

always that chicken and egg sort of thing
that has us wonder whether the songs come from

the life, or the life comes from the songs.
How else to make sense of this fishing trip

in which there's something fishy going on,
as the girl from Sevier County sings after the butterfly

has scrawled her name in pink across the screen?
I first came across her in a schoolyard joke

where, in the tub, she made islands in the stream,
the same punch line one white coat repeats

as the doctors at The Roslin name their clone.
You do the math — the udder cell, the egg, the embryo

that yields this ewe that survives seven years.
The transgenesis that makes of us surrogates

to a bit of fiddle, a bit of pedal steel.
How, like ungulates, we kick it off right and kick

up our heels somewhere between 'I Saw
the Light' and 'I'm So Lonesome I Could Cry'.

Columbo

In my beige raincoat and my rattling car
I go back to where a plain-clothes officer chalks
a line around the remains of the crime writer
or the nightclub owner, and a flashbulb goes off
like a shooting star. I'll try one line of inquiry
or another on the fitness guru who thinks me
a buffoon, or the famed architect, brusque
with my questions about blueprints and flying buttresses.
Some inkling of the truth I will discern by the way
he turns his tumbler of bourbon, or how a cigar
seems to quiver in his grip. A tremor of the lips.
A twitch of the right eye. It all comes down
to what I read between the lines. After a while
the holes in an alibi will show like the work
of moths on wool. Say a man is in a room but he wants
someone to think he's in another room —
this magician, for instance, who's knocked off his boss
smack bang in the middle of his routine,
or the psychiatrist whose benign Dobermans
savage the associate who slept with his dead wife.
A car goes off a cliff, a barbell snaps a windpipe,
and I look past defective brakes and misadventure.
There's a key in the letterbox or under a plant pot.
There's a door left ajar, so I let myself in.
I play the acolyte, the smitten, slack-jawed fan,
trying my card trick against the master's sleight of hand,
watching the screen convinced the heroine
has reprised her role to carry out a crime.
I look for signs — a burn mark on a wrist that leads
back to spilled coffee at the scene, the car stereo
tuned to a classical station while the glove box
is all country & western. I sense a history
the suspect wishes to shake, like this new coat
I've been trying to lose for days. It keeps showing
up in the precinct's lost and found. I leave it

on the front seat with the windows rolled down.
If anyone tries to take it, I tell the dog, just look
the other way. Often it comes down to technology,
a typewriter ribbon on which, in negative,
the words of a letter remain, the electrocardiogram
that marks a change of heart from slack
to stress. Something amiss leads back to the empty bottle
wrapped in a white towel, or the struck match
that startled the gasoline. All brass and strings,
the theme tune plays as I walk the perp out of the scene
past the names of co-stars and story editors.

The Hypnotist

Everything happened
on the count of three,
or with a sharp click of the tongue.
In your left hand

you hold a *World Encyclopedia*,
he said, attached
to your right thumb
is a helium balloon.

Everything happened
at the snap of his fingers
as twenty of us
were whittled down to ten.

Remove from your pockets anything
that could be broken, he said.
Take off your glasses
and spit out your gum,

the music turning
new age and ambient
as we entered the swamp
and swim of the right brain.

There's a string attached
to your neck, and I'm pulling it, he said.
We're at the beach, he said,
let's have some fun.

We sank our feet deep
into the sand of it.
We licked the ice cream
that ran down our arms.

Since we were in a donkey race
we made the donkey go faster.
It was the sort of race
that anyone could win.

One of us lip-synced to Elvis,
another was struck dumb
as our master's voice ticked
like a metronome.

The floor is covered
with cockroaches, he said.
The more you kiss the bird
the more valuable it becomes.

We were small farmers
of small town America
closing our fists around
the udders of the air.

We were aiders and abettors
of the infamous shoe thief,
covetous of the high heels
worn by a neighbour.

I'm going to shoot you
with my tickle gun, he said.
He said, you're a goldfish,
and sure enough it happened,

as it happened that we
became Cold War spies, ballet
dancers to his *jeté, jeté,*
a troupe of Chippendales

stripped to the waist
but unable to remember our names
as we sang to celebrate
our shared birthday.

At the Reading

The men wore patches on the elbows of their blazers.
The women wore bright scarves.

Before we got started there was much bluster and flarf
about the death of print, the dearth of audience.

Between our esteemed readers there was a game
of who's on first, who's on second

that almost came to blows until someone flipped a coin.
In God we trust. *E pluribus unum.*

When the hostess blew into the microphone there was
    feedback
and a minute electric shock for her top lip.

Then the first of them stepped up.
How could he ever live up to his blurb's hyperbole?

For sure, the cook was in cahoots with the butler there.
For sure, the stable boy was sleeping with the maid.

All night the old tropes calcified into the new clichés,
those red-hot ironies and lemony conceits.

So many miles there were on the clock already.
And the parking lot was full of jalopies.

Statler and Waldorf

More and more the discourse moves away from us,
as with that idyll of a time, perhaps illusory,

that was ours and ours alone, the tie and top button
of where it all began, the tuning fork,

the silver spoon that segues to our colloquy
and critique up here, where we attempt to sort

the Gorgs from the Doozers, just a couple
of financiers near dotage eager to see how

the farce unfolds on set, even if, in the end-up,
we must accept we're just like all the rest

of these Muppets, and not much more
than foam rubber dressed in a doll's clothes,

our basic skeleton the selfsame unseen hand
that, in the pit, strikes up the band, has the cast sing

'Why Can't We Be Friends?' or 'Take a Chance',
whatever number sets in motion the whole shaboogie

and shebang, which seems chaos at first,
then takes a form, adopts the week's loose theme,

a murder mystery or a camping trip, into the seams
of which are sewn some ongoing intrigue

or running gag, the on/off romance of a pig and frog,
or the hapless bear in the polka-dot scarf

trying his latest sad excuse for a stand-up routine
against our nudge, wink and guffaw, one

of us playing the wiseacre, the other the straight man
as we man the border only the likes of us

can still discern between high and low culture,
even if a civil servant singing the Pest Control code

in the key of F is as heady as it ever gets round here,
where, whether our guest-star mimes perform

'Robots Having Breakfast' or 'Cowboys Playing Cards',
we end up with the same spilled milk and cereal,

the blush in our cheeks starting to reveal
a little too much midweek red meat and rosé

as we do our best to keep buoyant this economy
of laughter and applause, what began as sketch

and storyboard become this smorgasbord
that, in the end, will have us all speaking Swedish.

Plectrum

Or pick, quick
between
one finger
and a thumb,

what strums
the strings,
catgut or
nickel-wound,

sounds off
in the sound box
the chord

that other fingers
struggle
to hold down.

The Hucklebuck

for Billy

Before I let him rest, feet up and out of luck, pressed and
      impressive
    in his Sunday suit, his patent leather shoes, I want to
        frame my uncle
doing the hucklebuck at my brother's wedding, or whatever
      the dance
    at which he first lifts and twists and shimmies with my
        aunt. Perhaps

it's The Orchid, perhaps The Orpheus, where The Royal
      Showband
    have just pulled up to a side entrance in their
        Volkswagen van,
the numbers and letters on its red plates back to front. They
      unpack
    from its flight case a Lambeg-sized kick drum. The
        valves in their amps

glow like a Calor stove as they soundcheck, testing the
      microphone,
    one two, one two. The shape the singer's shadow throws
        over the floor
is animal. A giddy chimpanzee. A dancing bear. Later my
      uncle will
    show me how to throw the shapes of three chords on
        the fretboard

of his nylon string guitar. 'Enough,' he'll say, 'for "That'll
      Be the Day"
    or "Love Me Do".' But for now we follow him to where
        a girl

he's never seen before sips orange juice, or where his tie
         and top
      button come loose while the teacups quake on their
         saucers and,

atop the uncut cake, a plastic bride and groom seem ready
         to cut in.
      According to one definition the hucklebuck's a red-
         neck or a hillbilly,
either Amish or Pennsylvania Dutch. In another it's a tryst
      in which
      one party arcs her spine to let her partner in on where
         he'll wiggle

like a snake or waddle like a duck. The syntax of it must be
         given time
      in that incensed bedroom, or where the dry ice plumes
         like smoke from
the pack of Rothmans, Dunhill, or Superkings he'll make a
      chain
      with later, home from the nightshift to a taped episode
         of *Cheers*

or *Hill Street Blues*. My uncle, whose name becomes a
         wound the deeper
      I look into it. But for now the band, all Brylcreem
         quiffs and matching
suits as he extends his open palm, the lifeline a river, and the
         singer sings
      'Now here's a dance you should . . . ' For now, my
         brother led by his bride

towards the floor to dance a dance he liked to dance when
      he was four.

A lift and a twist. A shimmy and a kick. The record
turns like a corkscrew.
The singer gyrates his hips while a few miles away some-
body strikes
a match and lights the doused cloth that brims at the
bottle's open mouth.

In one photograph the Royal pose before the buffed
chrome of a ribbon
microphone, all flared, florid collar and gap-toothed
grin. In another
they rest one elbow each over an upright Baldwin and lean
in, as if
about to sing 'Kiss Me Quick' or 'If I Didn't Have a
Dime'. Sometimes

I mistake them for the Miami and, sure enough, here they
are, airbrushed
before a pool in Florida in their too-tight swim trunks
and Day-glo tans.
But for now, the far side of the border, the B-side of 'I Ran
All the Way
Home', my aunt and uncle limber under the spots and
strobes. For now

my brother slipping his love's hold and sitting down to
another egg
and onion sandwich, a glass of champagne. The flame
that is an ape amok
as it rips up the carpet and swings from the drapes.
As the band
burn down the house a house burns down, and my
aunt and uncle move

south to the planned town at the river's open mouth, where
        his fingers
    on those catgut strings are shadow animals. 'G' like a
        billy goat. 'A'
like an ox. The syntax of it must be given time. You push
    your baby out,
        you pull your baby in. You clip your nails, wait for
            your fingertips

to harden. You see the Miami stopped on their way home
        by men
    dressed up, but not for Halloween, the band still in
        matching suits,
hair still Brylcreemed, as they're made to stand in line.
        How, when one
    callow member of the gang points his gun, his thumb's
        a stray dog's

pricked ears, his forefinger its upper jaw. You see the beer
        cans bound
    to the back bumper as your brother and his wife veer
        off into a future
that takes the shape of shadows thrown on a blank wall, the
        swish
    and splinter of the mirror ball as it falls and shatters,
        and your uncle joins

the singer and the trumpet player. A lift and a twist and the
        coffin lid
    is shut on another wake you're too distant to attend.
        The lights come up
and the dead leave behind the flat line of a silence in which
        a lone figure
    gathers the empties and, with a dustpan and brush,
        sweeps up the butts.

Shannon

The river in spate, the planes going out and in
               and, in the blood, something alive like want
or homemade wine, or an eel trying to find
         its way back home.

It's all so black and white and flickering.
               It's all so sepia, all so pristine —
the green where we dropped coats to make goalposts,
         the tent we pitched beside

the airport fence. We stand in line, help pick
               the captains who pick teams, or we smoke
stolen cigarettes and dream of girls.
         We perfect the fine art

of the slide tackle and name the places
               we'd like to put our hands. Nutmeg and head rush.
Fly goalie and smoke ring. It's all so far
         away from what will be —

a tear in the reel, a tear in the myelin
               sheath that could mean, as well, lupus
or Lyme disease. And my cousin's new illness
         without clear source,

like the eel Aristotle believed born
               from a mud-nothing. From the flecks of scale
and skin scraped off on rocks, Pliny contends.
         From the gills of other fish,

or a blade of grass, dew-sodden in late May.
               How pastoral, this longing for the past,
its brave stretch of fair days, river in spate
         that enters ocean here,

rushing stolen shopping carts, scraps of cars,
       the hungry mullet venturing upstream, bottom
   feeders just like me. I take off my socks
       and shoes. I dip my feet.

How the eyes widen in this dim blue light.
       How the skin turns pale again in this pure cold.
   And the mind, aching for its own Sargasso,
       a disease of the muscle,

autoimmune. We drink dandelion wine
       and hurl into the toilet bowl. We dream
   of some Russian air hostess undressing in
       the dark behind the eye.

No sign yet of what might soon transpire
       as a stasis in the limbs, the tongue turned stone,
   double-vision, as memory has it most of the time,
       the planes going out and in,

something alive in my cousin's blood, quiet,
       determined, not to be stalled by weir or waterfall —
   eel that will eat its own body almost whole
       as it returns to source.

Gospel Caravan

Of temperance, they come to talk to us
from *The Book of Romans* or *Leviticus*,

of hellfire and brimstone, dust and ash,
as the photographer stoops to ignite the flash

and bring forth, from the outskirts of Strabane,
their faith mission, their Roma caravan

pulled into the roadside, the steps let down
to where time frames them in the here and now

of the Titanic and 'A Soldier's Song'
before Passchendaele, or is it the Somme,

calls one of them to step out of the shot
and swap his bible for a bayonet

and put his helmet on, or so you guess,
something in his stance seeming to suggest

a cropped future. The way, as if they're tied,
he holds his hands behind his back. Those eyes

that read condemned above that stiff moustache.
The footboard he stands on like a scaffold

around which we're arraigned. Whether we long
for a neck snapped to right some fêted wrong,

or for the bluster of a pulpit sweat,
we push forward, step towards the spectacle,

desperate to climb those steps, to work ajar
that little curtained door, bowing to enter

an interior, where the ornery line
of the unknown might once have been divined

by way of tea leaves or an open palm
opened here to show us the end at hand

as, in their donkey jackets and neckties,
they make of us evangelists of light

and shade, and tattered tree, the one, two, three
the man who stands behind that mute machine

counts up while they hold their staunch pose
and the shutters of the eye open and close.

Double Exposure with Spirit Photographs and Summer Job

In the pocket of my porter's uniform I kept it like an
    amulet, a lucky charm —
    that glass bauble cut to a fake diamond from the
        chandelier's suspended midair
shower. Trinket. Gewgaw. Ersatz harbinger. I turn it over
    once more in my palm,

        finger and thumb it until it breaks the skin. I climb the
        wobbly stepladder again
with my Windowlene, my bucket of used towels — details
    that might help frame me
    in that place, that time, which is Eastbourne, which is
        the century's wrong end,

a striped deckchair and a melted ice-cream cone, our maitre d'
    who came
    from Krakow or Poznan, trying his tongue around
        'another day, another dollar'
as we wash our hands before the same crooked mirror on the
    ground floor

        of The Mansion. All this week I've been trying to make
        sense of *Leviathan*,
Hobbes's lush and rambunctious sentences, his conception of
    how memory
    makes, of each of us, a girl sweeping a hotel room in
        search of a lost earring,

a lost pearl; how memory makes, of each of us, a Springer
    Spaniel ranging
    the field until it finds the scent. All this week I've been
        staring at images
in which, some sleight of hand, trick of the lens, the dead rest
    their wet palms

on the shoulders of the living, all slicked back hair and
    hats, and Sunday best,
the photograph a means by which they might let us know
    they continue to exist.
    And so, the lost wife who shows up behind her bereft
        husband. And so, the son,

much missed, come back from the front on Armistice with-
    out a scratch. Like
    this, the past creeps up on the present. Light of a
        sudden where no light had been,
a face rising from silver salts and gelatin to cleave the air
    above the cenotaph.

    A secretary conjuring out of your grief, the clippings
        from a magazine, the cut-
and-paste figure of a lost love. Call it the catch and drag of
    pure fancy, a man
    running over the alphabet in search of an apt rhyme —
        like a blue-arsed fly,

the eye alights on the carcasses that sway in the coldroom,
    on the kitchen
    where my friend, the pearl diver, dips through soap
        suds for knives and forks
and spoons, while the breakfast chef, an ex-merchant sea-
    man, divides us,

    Paddy from Taff and Pole from Czech. Once more I
        rise and fall between floors
with the equine features of the night porter who could hear
    the dead whisper
    and bitch in the elevator shaft, who could see them
        wander the early morning

corridors looking for something lost, something mislaid.
Once more I bear,
down or up the backstairs, a plate of toast, touched or
untouched, a glob of butter,
for our most famous guest, a mid-ranked tennis player
who's lost once more.

I can hear the ball as it snags in the net cord, its pock
against the racket's mesh
of strings, the umpire saying 'Sir, please sit down so play
can resume.' I can taste
salt spray, warm English rain, a whole world opening at the
prompt of my tongue

with something like the same shattered longing that might
raise the dead, settle
them in the frame, double-exposed. Think Hobbes's
idea of the centaur as a man's
body superimposed, by memory, over the body of a horse,
of how the past is

a circle we can't square. Think of the mothball and
blue-rinse old dears laying
down, one over the other, their chested cards in the ball-
room's crushed splendour,
a nighttime game of gin. The eight, nine, ten of hearts.
The jack, queen, king.

In the Butterfly Garden

Here is another hive the eye
        might fly into, another place
    I'd like to put my hands,
as if the heart were wings at work
        behind this chicken wire, as if this skin
    and bone were apiary,

when really we're archaeopteryx
        at best, cuckoo maybe, or the man
    who dances on the Isle of Rum
among the gulls. With his rucksack empty
        but for a set of maps,
    a length of rope, he's come

by ferry and by train to claim
        the eggs he'll stash in his bed frame,
    or a box in the attic, just as we've
come along the interstate, past
        the Yankee Candle and the Red Roof
    Inn, for the small postman

and the ghost brimstone, the cloudless
        sulphur and the dusky swallowtail.
    And I'm thinking of the day our son
slid from your womb, after our mid-
        night drive, the emergency room
    that reeked of booze and sweat

and iodine. After your wish
        and push, your water's broken, how
    his head smelled of the sea, how
to hold him was to hold my own
        heart in my hands, startled, newborn,
    as one of the experts

here holds a warbler or a thrush,
          lifting it from palm to palm, saying
    'up, up, up'. Your first glimpse will be
one of awe, the guidebook instructs,
          and after, what? The hissing cockroaches
    in the next room, the koi

pond where the fish are too obese
          to swim? It's what's engrained
    in each of us, our egg lover insists,
this need to want and keep, to have
          and hold, who learned to scavenge first
    in bombed-out lots,

then in the nests of dotterels
          and choughs, who knows better than us
    what makes the old dear with the walking
frame, the sagging arm tattoo,
          wait to take, from your finger,
    a fig-tree blue, or

a blue diadem, and how the heart
          flails as it falls through space and time.
    Next it's our boy who tugs your arm.
He wants a butterfly he can take
          home. In his fedora and pink Crocs
    he wants to trap a bird.

At the gift shop we'll buy him off
          with stickers, a magnifying glass,
    and a pack of playing cards in which
the queen of spades is the mountain
          Argus, and the king of clubs
    a common jezebel.

Conventions of the Power Ballad

To every rose its thorn, to every bird
the broken wing we take up in our hands
and try to splint. Because the heart is half
and half again, a lighter held aloft,
its flint burning the skin. Because the heart
is dark and chambered like a gun, guitar
solo, the susurrus of drums, the ex
that marks the spot we dress up in spandex,
a poodle perm. The heart all arms and legs,
fingers and thumbs, the most and yet the least
abstract of nouns. What it is, what it wants
beyond our ken. Unless it's sonnets,
unless it's silicone, and candles in the wind,
the heart all sediment and sentiment.

John Peel Mixtape

Frequency and wavelength. Static of the in-between.
Like a telescope the antenna opens towards where

the song begins. Whatever seaside dive or bedsit room
in which my finger hovers over a record button

red as the wedding suit you wore in homage to
your favourite team. I press down again on where I am

some phrase or other lost in a scratch on the last track,
side two, or a mixtape come unspooled and wound

like tinsel round the sprocket-shaped fir trees,
where these days my father hangs up giveaway CDs

to keep the blackbirds from his raspberries.
Xmal Deutschland. Alternative TV. A festive fifty

at the arse end of the eighties. At number forty-three,
The Mega City Four. I check the mirrors and reverse

towards where you've pulled the car over to the shoulder
to listen in as that ex-choir boy from Rosemount

sings of his teenage dreams. And isn't it about time
we heard again the best record in the history of the world?

That kick and snare count in. That chord sequence.
A first line you would choose as your last line.

All of those Friday nights I set the dial and waited
for you to fill the room with sound. Collateral

and, yes, incompatible. Sham 69. The Desperate Bicycles.
Another session by The 'mighty' Fall. Mark E Smith

stalking the live room like a starved animal
before he smacks the drummer and sacks the band entire.

I spike my hair with egg whites and icing sugar.
I put on my hair shirt and my winklepickers and step

to where I am once more half man, half biscuit,
and all I want for Christmas is a Dukla Prague away kit.

Elegy for the Oatfield Sweet Factory

Obeying the tongue,
parsing the heart's
grammar, any of
several prepositions
might set you here,
between the mental
and the general
hospitals, the not
yet derelict factory
just down the hill.

Some loved thing
dies and we pass it
through the fire
or send out for a mass card
and a bouquet. Some
loved thing dies
and leaves us standing
in the breakdown
lane, one thumb
outstretched toward
the oncoming cars.

And nothing yet stopped,
not yet invited in,
we contemplate
the nomenclature
of the Eskimo Mint,
a hand sunk deep
into the soft pocket
of what's no longer there
for an Emerald,
or a Winter Easer.

Nostalgia

Always the rain, always the cloud
    cover, the peaks and troughs,
the closing isobars, the north by
    northwest tilt of the vane's arrow,
the needle pert in the hygrometer.
    Always the three-piece funeral suit
you wear, a scrunched up cigarette
    in one pocket, a bent nail in the other,
and the glass-rim hum of voices
    in the high wires, where crows
congregate like boys on a corner.
    You feel your way back blind
towards somewhere, no white stick,
    only the tips of your fingers. You slip
between the lines, go limber, then
    limbo beneath the caution tape
around the scene. Always the diesel
    fumes. Always the waiting room
of pneumonic coughs and scattered
    newspapers, the destinations listed
over the counter where you slide
    a crumpled note into the trough,
collect your ticket and change.
    Always the hiss of the pneumatic
doors before you board, the driver
    squat amidst his gadgets and gears,
the floor viscous with piss and vinegar
    as you step into the aisle, its seats
held together with masking tape
    and chewing gum. On each arm-
rest a flip-top ashtray like an urn
    that carries the stubbed-out remains
of every boy you've ever been.
    You lose the run of yourself again,
slip backwards, the past, the future

like two subway cars almost touching
in the cryptic dark of some faraway
    metropolis, the passengers like fish
against the glass. Smoke wafts
    from somewhere, or a throwback
hit bursts from the subwoofers,
    and you hear the screech of air
in the airbrakes, the uphill, downhill
    shift of gears, as you pass through towns
nondescript and scripture. Betting
    shop. Chip shop. Post Office. Bar.
The Mountaintop a stating of the obvious.
    The Dew Drop Inn perhaps a slurred pun.
The wreck of a Cortina or an Escort
    Mark I set up on blocks in a garden,
where someone's improvised a coop
    for chickens, or a kennel for a dog
with two different coloured eyes.
    There are the doughnut shaped skid marks
of the boy racer at a crossroads
    that opens four ways into nowhere,
and the phone box lit up at the corner
    like a spaceship that will never take off.
There's the ghost kiss of the cue
    off the cue ball in the snooker hall,
long abandoned, and the milk bottle
    vase of daisies and dandelions
below the palms of the blue-robed
    virgin at her roadside shrine. It's never
not this way, what you're trying
    to get back to, like the TV
on mute in a room just off the bar,
    where *The Angelus* drones on forever
and ever and the owner waits
    for the bell above the door. One

Russian nesting doll inside the other,
     you make a paper chain of figures
joined at the ankle and wrist,
     the game you're playing a game
of snakes & ladders. Always the yes,
     no, yes, of the wipers. Always
your falling asleep against the pane
     as you get lost again somewhere
between reverence and blasphemy.
     Always the radio soundtrack, the static
of the years. Always the burned rubber
     and spilled beer, the country singer
packing up his gear before the chintz,
     wince, speed rinse of techno from
the disco next door, someone throwing
     a fish supper up over his own shoes
as all your old selves square up to
     each other after last orders, the barman's
fourth or fifth 'Time now, folks, please'.
     Always the closed fist, the skinned
knuckles and loose teeth. The *are we*
     there yet? The *when will we be there?*

Flowers of Sulphur

You put your faith in a flat surface and time stopped in a line
as the tonearm dips to the record's outer rim

and the weather writes its braille across your skin,
gets its hands around your throat and won't let go.

Once more sound ripples up to bang its drums
with the endless chafe and thrum of what was once

but will never be again, those melodies and spoken sentences,
loops, earworms as you snap the past's wishbone.

'Are you wet?' your mother asks as you step in
out of the drench in your school uniform's sagging

mustard and green. 'I don't want to wake up
on my own anymore,' your favourite singer sings.

To cure what ails you you've tried onions, you've tried steam,
a grey-blue clay from Lourdes or Cahersiveen

that gave your face the grave smoothness of a death mask.
Akeley's gorillas or Keats by Gherardi.

Now this sallow powder you fix over a spoon,
wash down with water that tastes of bog and tin.

Killer of head lice and ringworm, ubiquitous cure,
how you need it, head-sick and heart-sore,

your skin all pocked and puce, a strange new moon.
Your skin raised text you read like a blind man.

You run your hands over its grooves. You test its grain.
Up to the mirror you hold a gaze no more your own

than your sister's pink hairbrush into which you sometimes sing.
You think you suffer and that your suffering

is for something, bottle of bleach, packet of razor blades,
props for a play in which you've fluffed your lines,

and so many the ways you've tried and failed,
and failed and tried, to hold onto what wants to slip away,

cutting its hurt and hover into glass, beeswax
mixed with a cold pint of gasoline, or this slate

and shellac medium the needle opens like a vein
to rekindle some cough or expletive, some heave of breath.

The Boxing Club

For the umpteenth time I chose the skipping rope
over the rope-a-dope that went on in the ring.
On the rubber soles of my Nike Air Force 1s
I rose and fell, I learned my feet had balls.
Ciotóg they called me and later cack-handed
when I learned to play the upside down guitar.
Who I wanted to hit, or who'd hit me, I don't remember,
but I was no pugilist, that much was clear.
At the centre of our thrown together gym
the real contenders sparred — those brothers Grimm,
those brothers Karamazov, who on weekends
fought outside The Pier or The Lagoon.
'Would you like to dance?' was their favourite pickup line.
'For Whom the Bell Tolls' was their favourite tune.

You're Not as Green as You're Cabbage Looking

I know now that my aunt's favourite tipple
        translates as Aunt Maria
    and that the catchphrase in that old radio jingle
meant eat a little girl today,
        as if to say language
    makes of us all cannibals,
or food, how in Berlin the mood lightens
        at the sudden slip of tongue
    that turns to a jelly doughnut
    the world's most powerful man.

In another lexicon you could live
        a second time. You could own a horse
    you took to the beach at the weekend.
Like the girl I sat behind in Honours French
        Je suis allé à la plage avec mon cheval,
    though I could never imagine
how any of us, all grey and maroon,
        all waiting to go up the town lunchtime,
    would ever need directions to
    Le Centre Georges Pompidou.

Le singe est sur la branche, the stand-up explains.
        In this routine he's trying to book a room.
    The punch line's all about utility.
Maybe the authors of that advert liked the rhyme
        of 'eat a' and *chiquita*,
    maybe they were a danger to children,
as so many were back then,
        the past always with a stick of rock
    in its raincoat pocket
    and a clutch of puppies in the Hiace van.

The curate stops to pick up again
        the same boy on his way home.
    They're going to the beach.
That man of cloth has promised him a horse.
        English was so full of exceptions
    and, to the non-native,
Irish too could present the odd problem.
        Tá an ceart agat and you had it right.
Tá an cearc agat and you had the hen.
Black was blue if we were talking about skin.

In the oral the *cigire* got me in a full nelson.
        I'd forgotten to take off my 'Free Mandela' pin.
    'You're not as green as you're cabbage looking,'
my mother would intone.
        It meant roughly the same as 'you're no goat's toe'
    and made as much sense
as my father's insistence that I 'put wood i' the 'ole.'
        Here was a man who could not tolerate a draft,
    although he'd left school at fifteen
    to apprentice with a draughtsman.

On his draughtsman's lamp I adjust
        the articulating arm to examine these blueprints
    that leave me with all of these loose ends.
There is only so much I can explain.
        Those advertising men, for instance,
    not a single word of Spanish between them.
Not a word of Spanish or a balls notion.
        They just want us to eat more bananas,
    and they might just kill us —
    all that potassium.

Twister

I was thinking of us spread arm over leg, spreadeagled
if you will, as we watched the sky turn green over a
    Carbondale

strip mall. In the Hunan restaurant we'd picked the red
snapper clean, leaving intact just the backbone, the head

and tail, as with the coin we might have flipped once in a
    basement
to settle who'd call the colours and who'd call the limbs.

We were one foot in the yellow, the other in the blue,
as the Doppler radar tracked the squall's latest moves

from the Storm Center in Norman, Oklahoma, its cut
and thrust putting us in mind of that thirty-five-foot

twister of muslin and chicken wire that, in Kansas, in 1939,
would touch down soon on the Gale family farm,

where Uncle Henry and those three shiftless farmhands,
who will become the Scarecrow, Lion, and Tin Man,

try to stop the horses from bolting before bolting up
the barn. As it is when Dorothy — played for a few shots

by Bobbie Koshay and not Judy Garland — throws open
    the door
on Munchkinland, we'd stepped from sepia to technicolour

by way of tea-smoked duck, a little too much plum wine.
It was all painted backdrop, all artificial flower and vine

when you yelled out 'right leg' and I answered 'green'.
We both waited for the other to topple onto an elbow or
   a knee

as the updraft passed through Jonesboro or Pinckneyville,
gathering to its core a rowboat, a rocking chair, a woman
   on a bicycle.

Entering the Town of Ovid

We were somewhere to the north of Ithaca
when the phone went off, came alive in your lap,
the GPS getting us lost once more
and the voice down the line about to sex
the poppy seed, the lentil, the chickpea
grown in your belly to the size of a Key lime.
'You are entering the town of Ovid,'
read the sign, our boy becoming eyelid
and fingertip, shifting shape in the brine.
The cells, at their easy math, were busy
as he climbed the rungs of his double-helix,
stealing a trick out of *The Metamorphoses*.
Then we lost satellite and checked the map
between Lake Cayuga and Lake Seneca.

Glossolalia

Now that we're comatose
and ghost apocalypse,
now that our curiosity
has taken us to Mars,
and tracked by satellite
to this handheld device,
we firefly the want
and wish of where we are,
our soundtrack a little
elevator muzak, our soundtrack
'Let the Bodies Hit
the Floor', now that
we're hazmat suit
and unmanned drone, riding bareback,
guiding the Hummer home.

So much of it a waiting
for the file to load,
so much of it a sifting
through the spam, now that
our browsing has a history
that's traceable, now
that there's a camera crew
in every room. We stick
to script, read from
the autocue. We leave
our brief message after
the tone. There is that lot
of us, all so luscious,
and all that we assume
you shall assume.

For a little cardio, a hamster
wheel in the basement,
for a little cardio, brick dust

and caffeine, now that
we're pyramid, now
that we're Ponzi scheme,
rehearsing, for a new reality,
the stand-up routine
and the slow jam. A Glock
in the glove box and
a console in the hand
as, through the goggles
of our night vision,
we save the world with
our opposable thumbs.

So much of it objects
in the convex, so much
of it hashtag and dash cam,
now that we're preapproved
and pay-per-view, now
that we're sound bite
and emoticon. Open the box,
undo the bubble wrap.
Are you looking for love?
Do you want fries with that?
Would you mind filling out
our brief questionnaire?
In this fortune cookie
of a life the objects
of your desire appear closer,

and a man is born to act,
not to prepare. So much
of it twerk and vamp,
the lip-sync of the karaoke
queen. So much the ping-
pong ball above the words

that scroll across the bottom
of the screen — a gloss-
o-la-la-la-la-la-la-lalia
of apex and root and midline
groove and hyoid bone.
Our soundtrack sample loop,
white noise machine. Our
soundtrack laundered,
like cash, through Auto-Tune.

Black Box

As mouth, as tongue, black box, remember us,
between a diphthong and a glottal stop.
Biting into a pretzel, or a peanut,
black box trap our voices in your black sounds.
Lend us your ears, speak well of us, black box,
from beyond the grille of your confessional,
as we speak to you in Yiddish and Urdu,
in our dozing off, in our undarned airport socks.
Black box, our seat belt signs flash on, flash off,
and the black cross our vessel casts, it casts
no longer on dry land. Across the screen
it moves, like a white hand. Through turbulence
we watch, at vanishing, its meagre line,
and we pray, black box, you'll intercede for us.

Acknowledgements and Notes

Acknowledgements are due to the editors of the following publications where a number of these poems, or versions of them, were published first: *AGNI, Connotation Press: An Online Artifact, Ecotone, The Irish Review, The Irish Times, jubilat, The Moth, Plume, Poetry, Poetry Daily, Poetry Ireland Review, Salamander, The Scores, The Southern Review.*

Many thanks to Peter Fallon and everyone at The Gallery Press, to my colleagues in the English Department at Trinity College in Hartford, Connecticut, and most of all to Hope, Leo, and Aengus.

For poem beginning on:

page 15 The Guido referred to here is Guido Anselmi from Federico Fellini's film *8½* (1963). The Daffy Duck cartoon is *Duck Amuck* (1953).

page 27 The detective in question is Agatha Christie's Hercule Poirot.

page 28 The quote, slightly adapted here, is from a 1964 interview with the band conducted by Maurice Smyth for UTV. (Smyth asks 'What sort of brand image do you feel your group presents to the average mums and dads of Britain?')

page 29 I'm grateful to Jerry Hopkins for *Elvis: The Final Years* (1980).

page 31 The line 'That's the way the mop flops' is spoken by Vince Everett, Elvis's character in *Jailhouse Rock* (1957).

page 33 The film referenced here is *The Bridge*, directed by Eric Steel (2006). The phrase 'you elements' is from *King Lear*, III.ii.16. The other quoted passages are from Jay Parini's *Robert Frost: A Life* (1999). The second of these passages has been slightly adapted. (Parini quotes Frost as saying 'I used to trail him everywhere, in the way a boy does.')

page 36 Lines 12 and 13 paraphrase lyrics from 'Something Fishy' from *Hello, I'm Dolly* (Monument, 1967). The phrase 'kick it off right and kick up our heels' comes from Parton's introduction to Ben Smathers and the Stoney Mountain Cloggers and Melvin Sloan and the Melvin Sloan Dancers on the February 18, 1988 episode of *Dolly!*

page 47   'I Ran All the Way Home' was the original A-side to the Irish release of 'The Hucklebuck' on HMV records in December, 1964. The line quoted at the end of stanza seven is from Brendan Bowyer's version of the lyric.

page 53   The photograph in question is by J W Burrows from 1912. It appears in *Shadows on Glass: A Portfolio of Early Ulster Photography*, edited by Brian Mercer Walker (1977).

page 55   Some of the photographs featured here were part of the exhibition *The Perfect Medium: Photography and the Occult* at the Metropolitan Museum of Art, New York (2005). The references to Hobbes come from 'Of Imagination', the second chapter of *Leviathan.*

page 58   Thanks to Julian Rubinstein for 'Operation Easter: The Hunt for Illegal Egg Collectors' which appeared in *The New Yorker* on 22 June 2013.

page 61   The documentaries *Turn That Racket Down* (1999), directed by Kate Meynell, and *The Story of the Undertones* (2001), directed by Tom Collins, were important to this poem.

page 67   The lyrics quoted here are from 'Asleep' by The Smiths from *The World Won't Listen* (Rough Trade, 1987). Akeley is Carl Akeley, the taxidermist and natural historian.

page 72   James A Fussell's article 'Special Effects in *The Wizard of Oz*' from *The Wichita Eagle* on 15 August 2014 was helpful to me here. This poem is for Hope.

page 75   Lines 27 to 30 are adapted from Section 24, line 48 and Section 1, line 2 of Walt Whitman's 'Song of Myself' (1892).